HOW TO TALK TO (ALMOST) ANYONE

ABOUT (ALMOST) ANYTHING

By Elaine Cogan

Published by

Wise Fool Press
an imprint of the Wise Economy Workshop, LLC
Cincinnati, Ohio

Illustrations created by Kathleen Deal for *You Can Talk to (Almost) Anyone about (Almost) Anyone* Published by Portland State University Press, 1982

Wise Fool Press

an imprint of the Wise Economy Workshop, LLC.

Cincinnati, OH 45241

www.wiseeconomy.com

Produced and printed in the United States of America

Print Edition ISBN: 978-0-9900044-6-2

Library of Congress Cataloging-in-Publication data available

Dedication

To Arnold

with much love and appreciation for your TLC these many years

-EC

Table of Contents

Introduction

" I'm scheduled to give a speech next week to the Bar convention about the breakthrough we made on our last case, but I suddenly have to fly out of town. Will you do it for me? I'll give you my notes.

I'm sure you'll be fine. Thanks."

Who can say no to the boss? Without much enthusiasm, you agree to be his substitute. But now that you have said yes, panic sets in:

> How can you keep faithful to his notes while converting them to your own presentation style?
> Will the audience accept you as the surrogate?
> What will you do when your mind goes blank?

I hope it is some consolation that you are not the only one who is uneasy when you have to give an oral presentation. In fact, in the 2014 Chapman University Survey of American Fears, public speaking was the most frequently cited fear, ahead of heights, drowning, and flying.[1]

While that may not make you feel better, you can be assured you are in good company.

Whether we have to make a presentation to clients, a report to shareholders, a pep talk to employees, an address to trade or professional associates, or a speech to the local Rotary, Kiwanis, or PTA—and whether we are novices or experienced—most of us face speaking in public with some level of apprehension.

---

[1] http://www.chapman.edu/wilkinson/research-centers/babbie-center/survey-american-fears.aspx.

Experienced and successful speakers realize that *subjects don't bore people. People bore people.* If listeners accept you as a credible carrier of information, they will believe your information and respond positively to your presentation.

Unfortunately, too many individuals who have extensive knowledge of a subject ignore this. They expect an audience to pay attention just because they know something that others may not. These speakers neglect to make the effort to learn how to present that information well. They mumble through 20 pages of single spaced text or fumble through a jumble of hastily assembled notes or poorly organized slides.

Their delivery is so poorly articulated or disjointed that listeners find it nearly impossible to follow... fidgeting with their electronic devices, or finding other ways to be inattentive. The sad result is that the speaker's important points are lost or misunderstood, leaving both the presenter and the listeners dissatisfied.

No audience wants a speaker to fail. They have given up their precious time to be there, and generally feel inherent empathy with the presenter, if they are met at least halfway. Moreover, some of them have been in the same situation and are likely to be inclined to be kind and accepting of some flubs or mistakes.

In the case of the inexperienced assistant referred to above, she still has time to perfect the presentation in her own style while keeping true to the major points the boss wants to cover. If she does not make that effort, her anxiety will be reinforced when she does not do well. She will learn a negative lesson: that she needs to figure out how to turn down any other speaking requests or demands without jeopardizing her job.

It takes an effort to learn to express ideas clearly and with panache and conviction. Very few of us are natural orators. We can, however, learn to give credible speeches, and that is what this book is all about. Help is at your fingertips!

To be a successful speaker, you do not have to enroll in a course in public speaking or read a 500-page tome. Just follow the hints on the following pages and you will enjoy the satisfaction of seeing your audience smile, nod in agreement, applaud appreciatively and envy your skill and aplomb. You may even enjoy the experience so much that you will look for more opportunities.

My first book on this subject, *You can Talk to (Almost) Anyone about (Almost) Anything*, was so successful that I have been encouraged to revise it in light of profound changes that have occurred in the workplace and new insights I have learned over time as a coach and consultant in oral and written communications. Unfortunately, Ben Padrow, my collaborator on the first volume, died several years after its publication, after enjoying a well-deserved reputation as the premier professor of speech communication at Portland State University and the coach of a wide array of successful political and business people.

I am a founding principal of Cogan Owens Greene, a consulting firm in Portland, Oregon. I have devoted my career to providing professional advice to hundreds of people in government and business. In addition to consulting, I produced and hosted a highly rated radio talk show on an NBC affiliate; wrote a weekly editorial column for *The Oregonian* and *Oregon Journal* newspapers; served as a political commentator on a major TV station and provided regular contributions to a national publication, *The Planning Commissioners Journal.*

I also have written two other books: *Successful Public Meetings* and *Now that you're on Board: How to Survive and Thrive as a Planning Commissioner.*

Although they are often still in the majority, the speaker's platform is no longer limited to white men, as more women and people with diverse backgrounds and skills take positions of leadership in all facets of society. While the advice in this book is necessarily general in nature, readers are encouraged to be aware of the special attributes they bring to the podium. Your uniqueness is your asset.

This book is organized so it can be read straight through or opened to the chapters the reader may find specifically helpful. If you want to know how to get started, turn to the chapter, *Putting it all Together.* If you need tips on how to use visual aids most effectively, refer to *Replace your Thousand Words with a Picture.* (Chapter5). I still refer to the *Failsafe Checklist* (Chapter 11), when I have to give a presentation.

Most importantly, I cannot stress more strongly that *We Cannot Not Communicate.* Everything we do and say conveys a message about who we are and what we know. With that realization, we can perfect the art of effective speaking and reap the rewards of attentive and appreciative audiences. We may even get to enjoy it!

Elaine Cogan

Chapter 1: Rules of the Road

In the chapters that follow, you will find specific guidance on how to prepare and deliver a winning oral presentation. First, however, consider these general principles.

√ **Put yourself in a positive frame of mind by starting out with confidence.** If you are being given the podium by virtue of your position, i.e. president, chair or department manager, you did not rise that high without being considered someone special who has a message to convey. If you have been asked to deliver a speech on a specific topic, someone believes you have enough experience and training to impart useful information to a particular audience. If you are making an important presentation to potential or current clients, you have been chosen spokesperson because you have valuable expertise or knowledge.

In other words, you can be confident you have something to say to an audience that is waiting especially to hear from you.

√ **If possible, choose the time of day to speak that suits you.** Are you a morning person who is at your best early and tends to wilt by noon or soon after? Is midafternoon when you get your stride? Evening? If you cannot give your speech at your most optimum time, know yourself well enough to prepare accordingly. For example, take a short walk before your talk to revive yourself, or eat a protein snack -- not a candy bar that gives you an unnatural and short sugar high, or caffeine-laden coffee or tea that tends to dry up your vocal cords.

√ **Remember that listeners have only one chance to understand what you are saying.** Unless the audience will need them to follow along a complicated subject, I strongly recommend giving out handouts after, not before, your presentation. You want the attention of the listeners to be focused on you, not pieces of paper. Even though computer wizards can produce compelling slides and electronic presentations, sooner or later you will be confronted with a machine that does not work properly or other glitches that will require you to rely on your verbal skills. **Be prepared by knowing your script well enough to go on unaided.**

√ **Help the audience keep track of what you are saying by numbering your points clearly**—*one, two* or *first, second.* Use expressions such as *next, now, since, moreover, on the other hand,* or *let's look at this subject another way,* to help them keep track mentally of your transitions and recognize when a new topic is being introduced.

√ **Speak in a conversational tone, but not at a conversational speed**. A good rule of thumb is that it should take you between 90 to 120 seconds to read text on a double spaced, typewritten page. Practice until you are comfortable at that pace. It is likely somewhat slower than your ordinary speech.

√ **Refresh yourself—and your audience—by carefully planned pauses.** A glass of water nearby is a handy aide...not only for your vocal cords but also when you need to momentarily find your place or emphasize a point.

√ **Do not hesitate to share your well founded opinion.** *It appears to me... From my experience...The facts show us...* For the brief time of your presentation, you are the expert. Accept that role and act the part-- but do not overact by saying something you cannot back up with solid information.

√ **Relate to the audience and show what a human being you are by inserting personal anecdotes where appropriate.** *Just last week this happened to me...To illustrate my point, let me tell you about my experience... By doing it this way, we found that...* If members of the audience can relate to you, they will forgive— and most likely forget—any inevitable flubs.

√ **Do everything you can to bridge the physical and psychological gap between you as the guru/expert and the audience as the uninformed receiver.** Use personal pronouns such as *we, us,* or *our.* Avoid *I* or talking down to the audience as *You folks out there.*

√ **Take advantage of the fact that the spoken word is naturally more informal than anything in writing by contracting and combining words whenever possible.** *We're* is better than *we are; won't* should be substituted for *would not.* There are times, however, when you will want to use more formal wording for emphasis. *We cannot do this* is much more compelling than *We can't do this.*

√ **As expert as you are, your points may have more weight if they are backed up by another authority who agrees with you. But choose the person or source carefully.** It must be someone who is credible to your particular audience. In general, the President's opinion is more convincing than that of Henry VIII, unless you are speaking to the Daughters of the British Empire or to members of the opposing political party.

√ **Avoid obscure or esoteric references that are tangential to your subject.** It may boost your ego to show listeners you know something they do not know, but they will not appreciate being reminded. Even though they are unlikely to show open hostility, audiences have a way of getting back at a speaker who talks above their heads and shows it. They will stop listening, respond with tepid applause, refuse to buy your product, not hire you or your company, or, worst of all worlds, never ask you to speak to them again.

√ **Use metaphors, analogies and anecdotes to lighten up your message**—but only when they are appropriate to the subject and suited to your style.

√ **Avoid the trite and often inappropriate opening joke.** No situation EVER reminds you of a funny story.

√ **Use exaggeration and hyperbole sparingly.** Words such as *magnificent, tragic, awful, greatest, worst, best* are useful, but only when you are making a special point that you can back up with evidence.

√ **Cultivate a rhythm and delivery that is pleasing to the ear and true to your style and personality.** Slow down or repeat an important point; use your fingers to enumerate ideas (*first, second and third*); lean forward conversationally. In other words, use mannerisms that are comfortable for you.

√ **Be assured that no audience wants a speaker to fail.** They most likely feel relieved they are not in your shoes.

√ **Honor the time limit by remembering one of the most important possessions of people is their time.** Use it wisely and they will return the favor by being attentive.

√ **When you accept the speaking engagement, offer to write your own introduction.** The moderator will most likely appreciate that this is one less chore for her or him to take care of before the event. Make it brief, but include information that best shows how qualified you are to speak on this given topic. Include a phonetic pronunciation of your name if it is difficult or unusual to pronounce. Take along a copy of your introduction in the likely situation the moderator may have lost the one you provided beforehand.

√ **People are persuaded by people first and then by information.** If the audience believes in you as a credible carrier of information they are most likely to believe what you say. Capitalize on this good will by being relaxed and confident. If you follow the steps in this book, you will be.

Chapter 2: Putting It All Together

In this chapter you will find everything you need to know to organize a winning presentation. Take these important first steps:

Analyze the audience. Even the best speakers fail because they do not take into account the expectations of each group. And each group is different.

Before you begin to decide what you are going to say, arrange for a phone or electronic conversation with your host. Ask about the size and makeup of the listeners. Is this the first time they will have heard about this subject or are they generally conversant? What do they most want or need to know?

Demographics are important also: Average age? Gender? Primarily women? Men? Mixed? Find out as much as you possibly can about each group to whom you are speaking. Then, armed with that information and your knowledge of the subject, you can feel confident you are the right person to give this presentation, at this time, to these people. Now, you can develop your message. Ideally, it is about three weeks before your scheduled presentation. If you have less time, you will have to work faster. If you have more than three weeks, put the speech in the back of your mind for a while, or at least try to.

Heed the advice that follows and you will compose a 20 or 30-minute presentation that covers all the material you need to say at this particular time for this particular audience. Do not plan to speak longer than half an hour, although the audience may keep you overtime with questions. The only instance I am aware of where length is rewarded and brevity is suspect is when academics talk to other academics. Most people are polite and will not just walk out on a speaker who goes overtime, but they will fidget, roll their eyes, and otherwise show their displeasure, regardless of how interesting you may be.

Take note that the attention span of the average adult is 2.5 minutes before the mind strays. That is why you need to divide your thoughts into short segments as you create your speech. Even if you are certain you have more information than can be conveyed in that amount of time, restrain yourself. After you are done, distribute the additional information as a handout that people can read at their leisure. Or, you may be so good the group will ask you to come back and you can present everything you left out the first time!

Save some of this additional information for the question and answer period, which you should consider a logical extension of your speech. A speaker who is not willing to answer questions is immediately suspect, as the audience wonders what he or she has to hide. Being willing to answer questions marks you as someone who has confidence enough to risk facing the unexpected.

But you will have that confidence—more on that in another chapter. I recommend a somewhat unusual way to compile your material, but it is a proven formula for success. This method has many advantages. Although the final presentation should have a beginning, middle and end, writing the speech in that order can stifle your creativity.

As noted above, you have already been in contact with your host and agreed to your general topic and the specific types of information most likely to interest this particular audience. This chapter assumes you will not be using any visual aids in your presentation. In Chapter Five, I explore how these can be used most effectively.

Jot down random gems

It is time to begin the three-week countdown period. Start by recording everything you know about the subject, without bothering with the order or the form. Your notes may look like a stream of consciousness of random ideas, but the important point is to get them all down. I find it useful to carry note paper and a pencil or pen so I can jot down random gems as they come to me. Some find it useful to put their ideas on notecards or use a note-taking app such as Evernote or Trello. Others scrawl on Post-It notes, paper napkins, place mats, or random scraps of paper. It is not important what you use, but it is important to capture all the brilliant ideas that pertain to your subject. For later ease of organization, limit your thoughts or pieces of information to one per note.

During this first week of your three-week preparation period, use your spare time to advantage by putting your speech-writing brain on automatic pilot so that it clicks on when you are engaging in routine activities -- riding to work, eating lunch, taking a shower, going on errands, waiting for your child to finish a music lesson or sports event. Your thoughts are wandering anyway; think idly about the contents of your speech and you will be surprised about how many good ideas will come to you. But be sure to write them down.

Next, assemble all those thoughts in a logical order. Spread them out on a table or the floor. This should be easy if each has been written on a separate piece of paper. If not, take the time to rewrite them. If you have kept your notes in an online tool, find the easiest way to organize them. Cutting and pasting is fine, but some people do better with an interface that allows them to move "cards" around. Scrivener, for example, is designed to allow writers to do exactly that.

Arrange and rearrange your collection of comments and ideas as you would a deck of cards, until they make the most sense. This should be fun as you see the appropriate organization emerge, and you may even have an "eureka" moment. Now you will understand why I recommend this creative process and why it works. It encourages you to pick up innovative ideas from a variety of sources, which in all likelihood never would have occurred to you if you had just gone about writing your speech routinely from beginning to end.

Next, divide all your notes into three piles: introduction, body, and conclusion. This should happen at the beginning of week two as you are ready to start composing, following the order I describe below.

As you write, remember that a speech is not a term paper. It is a special form of communication with its own rhythm and style. For example, contractions such as "isn't," "don't" or "shouldn't" are frowned upon in formal written communications, but commonplace, and often preferred, when making a verbal presentation.

Use short words and sentences and direct nouns and verbs. Avoid technical language and drawn-out descriptions unless they are pertinent to your subject and easily understood by your audience. Avoid buzzwords and garbled words such as *planning-wise, health-wise, and speech-wise.* More common versions such as *clockwise, otherwise and lengthwise* are fine.

Keep a dictionary and a thesaurus at your side or open in your computer browser. These are invaluable sources of pronunciation, as well as a help in expanding your vocabulary. At this stage in your speech writing, it is not necessary to be concerned with spelling, unless you will be giving away copies of your presentation, slides or other visuals. As noted in a subsequent chapter, accurate spelling and punctuation are essential on those documents, but not important in a speech for your eyes only. In fact, you may want to write out words phonetically that you are likely to stumble over or are difficult to pronounce.

Finally, putting pen or pencil to paper or fingers to the keyboard, begin to compose the body of your speech, followed by the conclusion or summary, and only then, the introduction. The latter should contain 'teasers" or snippets of information that will entice the listeners, while the conclusion is a logical ending to all you have said without adding any new information. Obviously, you cannot write those two sections until after you have decided on the body or main points.

Be somewhat ruthless in choosing only three key points to cover as the substance of your speech, remembering once again the limited attention span of your audience and your desire to keep them listening and focused on what you are saying.

Write your finale or conclusion with care. This is your last chance to impress your audience and you want to leave them with at least one idea or thought they will long remember.

Do not reveal that you are so relieved to be done with the talk by ending with, *I guess that's it, thank you and good day.* Even worse, do not bring up new or irrelevant material, adding lamely, *Oh, yes, I nearly forgot...*

Summarize the main points of your presentation (remember, only three), and add a personal touch or appeal for action that will stir your listeners: *This is why I volunteer for such a worthy cause...I truly believe this is the best course of action and I hope you will join me.*

Include a memorable quote or favorite stanza of poetry only if it is appropriate to your subject and you feel comfortable about it. If you never read Shakespeare—or you know your audience doesn't—do not trot out the Bard just to impress people. You will not.

Reject the temptation to conclude by thanking people for their attention. If you have been successful, they will thank you. If you haven't, don't remind them.

Before the end of week two, you should have completed two of the three sections of your presentation. It is time to prepare the introduction. The purpose of this part of your speech is to capture the attention of your audience, convince them you are worthy of being listened to, and lead them expectantly into the main part of what you are saying.

If you are sure of your information and it is appropriate to your subject and your audience, you may want to begin by being somewhat provocative:

Ten years from now, 20 percent of us in this room will have died or be seriously ill of cancer.

Or, with a question:

How many of you know that the United States has one of the highest infant mortality rates in the world?

Or with a story:

When I was growing up, I looked forward to a steaming bowl of oatmeal for my breakfast. Today, too many children are lucky to have dry, cold cereal.

Or a familiar quotation:

As Franklin Roosevelt said, 'We have nothing to fear but fear itself.'

Many speakers begin with fulsome praise, thanking the person who introduced them and saying how happy they are to be there. This is a nice touch, but be brief. If overused, it can seem insincere. Choose your words carefully and do not overdo.

Avoid comments such as *I don't know why you asked me to talk to you today —I'm not really a public speaker—I hope you will all bear with me.* We all have heard speakers who seem to think they must be super humble and apologize for everything—for just being there, for presuming to talk at all on the subject, for not being the Nobel Laureate on the issue. If you have nothing worthwhile to say, your audience will find that out soon enough.

Do not talk up or down to your audience. Use words you know they understand in the context they understand.

As I noted previously, be wary of telling a joke (*This reminds me of a story*) unless you are a recognized standup comedian or absolutely sure of yourself. It is likely to be unfunny, inappropriate and unnecessary.

Do tell personal anecdotes to which the audience can relate: *I remember well when I was a teenager and...*

If you are substituting for someone else at the last minute, do not whine: *I wish I had had more time to prepare, but I'll do the best I can at this short notice.* This disparages the organizers and panders to the sympathy of the audience. Take charge as if you would like nothing more than to be there at this time and place.

End your introduction by leading into the body of your presentation and reminding people: *I will cover three points today. The first is...*

Follow this same organizational process for a shorter talk, though you may want to cover no more than two main points.

It may come somewhat as a surprise, but having followed these rules, you have written your whole speech. It is 20 to 30 minutes long and well organized to say just what you want to say. The introduction causes the audience to sit up and take notice, the body gives them information they are not likely to hear elsewhere or, if commonplace, is presented in a unique way. The conclusion rouses them to action or gives them ideas they will long remember.

This is the end of week two of your three week preparation time. The final week should be devoted to practicing. If you have not already done so, contact the individual who invited you to speak and offer to send a biographical sketch to be used in introducing you. The individual probably will be very grateful he/she doesn't have to bother with this and you can tailor your introduction to the nice things you want said about yourself. Be sure to take a copy with you as it may likely have been misplaced.

Now, you should be eager to spend the rest of your preparation time reading over your speech and listening to what all your words actually sound like.

Chapter 3: Use It or Lose It

Most people deliver a speech either by reading from a manuscript or paraphrasing pertinent ideas from scraps of paper. The few who memorize the contents are most often salespeople who give the same presentation over and over. I personally find notecards to be the most helpful technique. They are easy to read and less flimsy than paper.

As you become an experienced speaker, I hope you will become adept at organizing your material into key phrases instead of complete sentences, still always divided into the introduction, body and conclusion discussed in Chapter Two.

Whatever your method of composing the text, the key to successful delivery is practice, practice and more practice.

The particulars of delivering a speech with graphical material such as PowerPoint or Prezi are covered in Chapter Five. For now, I assume you are speaking without visual aids. However, even if you are using them, always be prepared to speak well without them. As every experienced presenter finds out to his or her dismay, if anything can go wrong it will go wrong, especially when dealing with computer equipment or balky microphones.

Now, back to the presentation you have created, following the advice in the previous chapter. Ideally, this is the third week of preparation- a week or so before you give your speech. You have spent the first week gathering your thoughts; the second composing the beginning, body and ending; and you are now ready to perfect your delivery.

If you are using a script, number each page. Type your speech double spaced, bold, capital letters, in at least 12-point font on one side only.

Practice!

Never staple or bind the papers together. Practice until you can turn the pages as unobtrusively as possible, or ideally, push each one aside on the speaker's stand. Try to arrange to talk behind a podium or table wide enough to avoid dropping your papers on the floor. You minimize or eliminate this problem if you have written your presentation on easy-to-manipulate note cards.

Begin practicing by reading your entire text without stopping into recording equipment such as a tape player, the audio recorder on your phone or computer, or an MP3 player with audio input. You will probably have to slow down your normal conversational speed to about 170 words per minute. Use a timer if you have one. If not, a good rule of thumb is that one typed double- spaced page has about 250 words. Delivered at a speed that people can assimilate, one page should take you between 90 and 120 seconds to read.

Replay the recording as many times as necessary. Listen carefully, making changes to your script or notes that improve their oral quality. Consider these factors:

√   Are any sentences so long you stumble over them and the listeners may lose your point? Shorten them so they are clear and succinct.

√   Is your message getting bogged down by convoluted phrases? Add transitional words such as *and, and so*, or *moreover*.

√   Are you stumbling over big or unfamiliar words? Substitute simpler alternatives.

√   Be frank with yourself: if you were listening, would you still be paying attention? Would your subordinates? Your boss? A group that never met you before? If your answer is negative, revise the text accordingly.

On the positive side, listen carefully for special phrases or sentences that express well what you are saying. Keep them and add similar ones that enhance your message.

If you know someone who is an accomplished public speaker, ask his or her assistance to listen and give advice. Unfortunately, most spouses, partners, friends, junior staff, or colleagues are not useful if they are reluctant to speak frankly. They may be too critical, or not critical enough.

You probably are your own best judge. Make appropriate changes in the text that clarify your message and express just what you want to say in a way most acceptable to this particular audience. Capitalize, underline or boldface the ideas or phrases you want to emphasize.

Never use a word that is unfamiliar to you or that you have trouble pronouncing. You are most likely to flub it when you are in front of the audience.

Do not linger over unimportant words such as *the*, *a*, or *and* — never pronounce *the* as *thee* or *"a"* as a long "A". For smoother delivery, use conjunctions -- *they're* instead of *they are*, *we've* in place of *we have*.

Vary your pace. Speed up transitional or less important ideas. Slow down or even repeat to emphasize a special point. *I want to say this again: It is very important that we take action soon.*

Make note of places where gestures can make your speech more interesting and/or emphasize key points -- but make sure they are natural to you and fit your content. Practice in front of a mirror. If you can do it with ease, gesture or hold up an object that illustrates what you are saying. If any of this makes you uncomfortable or does not fit your style or personality, do not try to program yourself for this presentation. You will look as unnatural as you feel.

Avoid scratching your head, stroking your face, jingling keys or change in your pocket or doing anything that reveals your nervousness and annoys the audience. Remove any likely distracting objects and leave them in your coat or with a friend or colleague.

Time your speech so that it is no more than 30 minutes, and be ruthless in eliminating extraneous words and phrases or even whole sentences. If they still seem important, do not throw them away: gather them up to save for another speech or keep them in mind for the question and answer period that follows.

Listen carefully to the pitch of your voice. Keep it well-modulated and in the low range. High voices lack a sense of authority and can be irritating to listeners. Unless you are a trained singer, you cannot alter your natural pitch radically, but if you tend to squeak when you are excited or nervous, learn to keep those symptoms under control by following the suggestions in *Chapter Six, Antidotes for Wobbly Knees and Sweaty Palms.*

Likewise, lower your voice at the end of each sentence. Unless you are asking a specific question *(How many of us took the bus here today?),* do not raise your voice at the end of a declarative sentence. This is a bad habit many people use in their everyday speech and carry over to professional presentations. It makes them sound uncertain or immature.

As you rehearse, listen carefully to any "ah's" or "um's" you inadvertently insert when you are looking for the next word or phrase. They are very distracting to the listeners and lessen the impact of your message. To ward off such situations, practice until you can pause discretely, or take a sip of the water you always should have at your side. The audience will not notice this moment of silence and you will have bought enough time to move on smoothly without cluttering up your speech with distractions.

Become familiar enough with the contents of your introduction and conclusion that you can deliver them as close to verbatim as possible. Your message will be more effective and well received than if you start and end with your nose to the written word or note cards.

Rehearse your entire speech until you know it so well that you can look up at your audience more times than you look down at your script. But just as you probably wrote it in snatches, you likely do not have a large enough block of time to go over it more than once in one sitting. Take a few minutes whenever you can, but try not to let any day go by in this last week without reviewing at least parts of your presentation.

You have asked your host previously about the size of the room and other logistics. Try to practice at least once in that venue. If that is not possible, replicate that environment as much as you can. For example, you can simulate a podium with a pile of books, a microphone with a short statue or a lamp. If you are using presentation slides or other visual aids, always rehearse with them beforehand and bring your own equipment.

If you are speaking in front of a microphone, come early enough so you can test it with a helper listening in the back of the room. Make sure you can adjust it to your height easily and rehearse so there is no static or unnecessary noise and you can be heard with ease. Only the novice taps into the mike just before the speech and asks the audience, "*Can you hear me?*" You are not that novice.

A last point in regards to preparation: if you are tempted to consider the time and expense of videotaping a rehearsal, my advice is, don't, unless you are preparing to talk before a TV audience. There are at least three good reasons for this admonition. First, if you are not a professional who is accustomed to being on camera, you can be unduly distracted by the apparatus. Secondly, video tends to distort one's image somewhat and make us look heavier. Third, speaking on camera is an entirely different medium than speaking before a live audience, so practicing in this manner may not actually help.

On the other hand, if you are comfortable being on camera, this may be a helpful part of your preparation. In any case, do not spend a disproportionate amount of time rehearsing this way. Expend your energies practicing with a voice recorder and you will be on your way to success as a speaker before a live audience.

By following my advice and dividing your speech preparation chores into manageable segments—one week to gather your thoughts, another to write, and the last week to practice your delivery and make any necessary adjustments—you are on your way to making a memorable presentation. No need to panic; you are ready for your big day!

Chapter 4: The Joke Should Never be on You

Who are your favorite comedians or story tellers? Those with the most staying power are likely men and women whose experience or style resonates with you and others like you. Somehow, they have found a way to connect with an audience of strangers. If the speaker is very effective, we may even remember some of the most memorable lines. But even though they may seem easy, successful use of humor takes talent, thought and lots of practice.

Do not make the mistake of repeating any jokes or stories you have heard others tell unless you are super sure they fit your occasion and you have a foolproof ability to deliver. Given these caveats, most novice speakers would do well to steer clear of even trying, for the following reasons.

Giving a speech that involves humor or story telling involves some risk. First, it requires you to talk about something that is compatible with your personality and style of presenting that is at the same time likely to amuse the audience. It is far too easy to get that balance wrong. Second, it involves an ability to be somewhat informal without being silly. Finally, the humor must truly fit into your message and not be an obvious add-on.

People generally enjoy an apt story or joke. But if you are uncomfortable being somewhat informal or have never used humor well, do not feel compelled to try to fit it somewhere into your otherwise carefully crafted speech. It would be better for you—and the audience—to play it straight without the embarrassment of a story or joke poorly told. If, however, after some practice, you can be a winning humorist, take advantage of that skill and add it to your quiver of abilities.

While the joke or story must be appropriate to the subject or theme of your speech, it can be placed anywhere—at the introduction to catch the attention of the listeners; in the middle to enliven dry facts or figures; or at the end to create a good mood or feeling.

Never start by saying, *Being here today reminds me of a story.* Savvy listeners know it does not remind you of a story at all, but is more likely one you heard at work or at a party and are awkwardly trying to stuff into your planned remarks.

Most of us are not natural comics, but we are anecdotal people, and the most effective tales are those we direct toward ourselves. If your story is gently self-depreciating it can make people feel superior, reassured they would never be that careless or foolish. Done well, you can endear yourself to the audience who will relate to you as a person and heed your more serious message. Moreover, if it works, you will give the impression that even though you are well versed in your subject and seemingly self-assured, you also, like most everyone, have human failures or foibles.

There is a fine line, however, between gentle self-deprecation and embarrassing denigration. You know you are on the right track if members of the audience smile or nod reassuringly as if to say, *I understand; I've been there*. A story or anecdote works best if it is believable and helps build a bond between yourself and the audience.

The first time I was turned down for a job, I learned a valuable lesson that some of you may be able to relate to....

Or: *My children are probably like yours. They like to argue, and I don't always have the right answer. Over time, I have learned to....*

If you are critical of the educational system, you might start out with a remark that gets people thinking:

In my opinion, every American child should learn a second language...English!

It is okay to be nostalgic about the past but, keep it within limits:

Down on the farm, when I was a child, I learned my first lessons in making hard choices

is more effective than

The farm was a special place where I never minded doing chores because I knew my parents worked much harder.

No one will believe that one.

Never target a remark to an ethnic, racial, gender specific or religious group. Such attempts at humor are not funny, always in bad taste and the surest way to alienate your listeners. For the same reasons, do not adopt a dialect or a foreign accent that is not your natural speaking style. It will not make your comment or story funnier or more believable.

Resist the temptation to laugh at your own humorous aside, though you may smile in a friendly, knowing manner.

Do not tell a story or joke that you do not know perfectly without having to read it. Write it down word for word as part of your text, and then memorize it. Practice, especially the punchline, until you can deliver it perfectly and are not likely to forget it or stammer in a time of panic.

It is unwise to give a speech consisting of a string of jokes or anecdotes. Pepper your remarks appropriately where they fit. If the audience wanted to hear a bona fide comic, they would have asked for one.

Everyone but the most entrenched curmudgeon enjoys a good story or light humor, but not everyone can be an effective teller of tales. Know yourself well before deciding if you are comfortable with this style of presentation and compose and present your speech accordingly.

Chapter 5: Replace Your Thousand Words with a Picture

To paraphrase an ancient Chinese saying, one picture is worth 1,000 words. That is still true, but only if it is the right picture!

Today's audiences are accustomed to receiving much of their information from digital media where the visual impact is often as important as the spoken or written word. Speakers who are skilled in the use of graphical material have another tool to keep an audience's attention, increasing the likelihood their listeners will retain the message.

In the not distant past, charts and overheads were the graphical aids of choice. Today, while they are still useful in some circumstances, we can choose from a wide array of digital techniques to accompany a presentation, ranging from PowerPoint slides, photographs and charts to videos and animation. Studies show that people typically retain more information they see and hear than they do of information they only hear,[2] so we should use the tools available to us when we can – and when we can use them well.

If you decide to use one or more visual aids - and some speeches are fine without them - always remember their function is to *assist* you in presenting your message. They are *not* your message.

In the finite time you have to prepare your presentation, do not spend so much energy crafting the contents of the visuals that you end up making them the show. You are still the most effective carrier of your message,

---

[2] https://www.td.org/Publications/Blogs/Science-of-Learning-Blog/2015/03/Debunk-This-People-Remember-10-Percent-of-What-They-Read

and you must be careful to be supported, but not dominated, by any aids you choose.

An important caveat: In the life of every speaker there is a time when the power fails or other unexpected misfortunes occur. Always be prepared to make your presentation without any visual aids. In other words, have sufficient mastery of your material so you can go ahead without them.

Choose only the highest quality presentation techniques and materials. Likewise, bring all your own equipment and rehearse with it in the room beforehand. Control everything you can: make sure you have the power cord to your computer as well as a backup digital copy of your slides. It also will ease your anxiety if you have copies on a flash drive and/or a cloud server that you can log into from another computer if yours suddenly does not work.

In addition to your equipment you intend to use, bring extra projector light bulbs, extension cords, marking pens, tacks, tape and everything else you may need. Never expect your hosts to provide anything except a screen and the microphone, even if they volunteer.

Select your visual material carefully with these criteria in mind: the purpose of your speech, type of audience, the audience's level of familiarity with the subject, and the size and other features of the room. Most importantly, choose your visuals with *you* in mind. Never use any you may have borrowed, with which you are not entirely familiar or are only tangential to your message.

If you use text slides, express your most cogent ideas in phrases, not complete sentences. In general, the fewer words on a slide, the better. Treat them as an outline to guide the audience. Never, ever read the text slides word for word.

Do not use reproductions from books or reports, clip art or digital images unless they are easy to see when magnified on the screen. Images pulled from web sites can become blurry when enlarged, so make sure the resolutions are of the highest quality and will show up clearly when projected. A freehand drawing that is somewhat humorous can be more appealing to your audience than a chart with microscopic numbers or words. Give credit to the source of any visual you did not create personally. A small footer or text box is sufficient.

Do not use any material you know will not project well. You will insult or bore your audience by warning them *I know you can't read this, but...* before you read a text that they indeed, cannot read clearly on the screen for themselves.

Avoid the temptation to use visual material cobbled together at the last minute or borrowed from another presentation, just so the audience has "something to look at." They are there to hear you and your message, not to watch some unrelated screen show.

If you cannot visit the room before the presentation, always come early to make sure everything is in working order. Locate and turn on the electrical outlets and light switches. Go through a dry run before the audience arrives. Make sure you know how to activate the projector if it has a "sleep" mode, and that it is focused and not warped. If the image on the screen looks narrower at one end, look for the "keystone" adjustment mechanism on the projector or reposition it manually. If you are not entirely comfortable dealing with any of these mechanics, bring along an able assistant.

Ascertain that everything you project can be seen by people in the last row by turning on the projector and asking a colleague to sit back there before anyone arrives. Discard any slides that cannot be seen easily from that vantage.

Make certain you or your assistant know how to use the remote control for the projector, including how to advance and go backwards and how to toggle from the slides to a browser if you need to. In general, do not use a laser pointer unless you are positive you can direct it properly and not let it wander all over the screen, or even worse, into your eyes or someone else's in the audience. This can be more than awkward. It can be dangerous.

Always place the screen or chart in the front and center of the room. If you are using a pen or pointer, stand off to the side and face the audience. This may take some practice, as your natural impulse will be to address the screen, thus turning your back on your listeners. This not only blocks their view but breaks the personal relationship you need to maintain with the audience.

If you have a complex presentation or an assistant running the equipment, agree on a subtle cue, possibly a nod, to tell the individual when it is time to move to the next slide. It is important not to interrupt the flow of your presentation by calling out repeatedly "*You can turn to the next slide now...*"

In some venues, such as small conference rooms or those with insufficient electrical access, you may want to eschew slides in favor of an easel on which you place poster-sized graphics mounted on cardboard or foam core. If you choose that approach, use about half as many images as you would for a digital presentation. Make sure your easel is stable and your images firmly mounted. Number them discretely and keep them in the right order. Always use bold colors and easy to read print. Practice beforehand so you can move them from one to the next smoothly.

Handouts can be useful if you have points that you want the audience to remember. But unless people need to take notes, or the handout contains material that is necessary for the audience to understand your remarks during the presentation, do not give them out until you are finished. Nothing distracts everyone more quickly than the few who rattle pages to try to keep up. Attendees who are interested may appreciate being given a link to a web site where they can call up your presentation at their convenience.

If you are using the handout to accompany your presentation and the talk is an educational conference or workshop, provide sufficient room on each page for people to take notes. A clear signal you have too much text is if there is no room on the pages for these notes when you lay out the page at a size that allows people to clearly read the printed text on the slides. Include your name and contact information.

If you will refer to the handout during your talk, make sure your audience has it beforehand – either by giving it out as people enter the room or by leaving it on each seat before the meeting begins. If there are several pages, harken back to kindergarten days and print each on a different colored paper: *We're now on page three...that's the orange sheet.*

Always assume at least a third of the audience will lose or misplace the material. Have extra copies to give out upon request afterwards.

.

Visual aids can enhance and complement your presentation, but only if you coordinate them with your remarks and remain in control. They are not a shortcut to effective public speaking.

If you cannot produce a set that is high quality or are in doubt about your ability to use them well, don't. You still have your vocal gifts to carry you through.

Chapter 6: Antidotes for Wobbly Knees and Sweaty Palms

Public speaking inevitably involves a degree of spontaneity and unpredictability. It is a live situation involving real people, whose feelings and reactions never can be fully anticipated. In that way, it is the opposite of a movie or video, where the director or editor can make changes or eliminate glitches with retakes, cutting or splicing. When you give an oral presentation, any mistakes you make are right there for all to see and hear. On the other hand, if you do a good job, you reap instant approval.

No matter how well you are prepared, when the day, hour and minute finally arrive, it is natural to suffer from some or most of these symptoms:

- ✓ A tendency to gasp for air, certain that your lungs and salivary glands have long since stopped working properly.
- ✓ An overwhelming feeling of nausea or even a feeling that you may faint.
- ✓ A conviction that the thump, thump, thump of your heart can be heard by people in the last row of the audience.
- ✓ A certainty your hands are so sticky that, like Lady Macbeth's, cannot ever be wiped dry.
- ✓ A sense that you are a disembodied spirit with no idea of the words you are about to deliver.
- ✓ A nagging fear that your voice will come out at a higher pitch than normal, if you have any voice at all.
- ✓ A struggle to maintain good posture while keeping your legs from wobbling and shaking.
- ✓ A belief that the audience is out there somewhere, but you can see only an indefinable blur when you have the courage to look.

These are real symptoms that at one time or another can afflict even the most experienced speakers.   Even so, they need not be debilitating.

Borrow a note from winning football coaches -*the best defense is a good offense* -or from the Boy Scouts: *Be Prepared.* Know your speech so well that you have the confidence you can act quickly and assuredly to deal with anything unexpected that may happen.

If, you have followed my advice so far, you have written a well-organized, cogent, and interesting 20 to 30- minute speech and have rehearsed it sufficiently that you own it.

You are as ready to deliver your remarks as you ever will be.

When the time comes, it is not unusual to be somewhat nervous. In fact, if you do not feel a bit of anticipation, you will deliver a flat and boring presentation. Read on to learn how to get all those butterflies to fly in the same direction.

Control your environment. As noted in previous chapters, if at all possible, check out the room a day or so beforehand. At the very least, come early so you can change what needs to be changed and accommodate to any unforeseen circumstances.

Unless the room is an auditorium or classroom with fixed seats, rearrange the seating to your liking by putting the shortest possible distance between you and the audience.

Lower or raise the thermostat, adjust the podium and the microphone to your height and make sure it is working. Arrange to have any canned music turned off. If you are using visual aids, find the electrical outlets and bring along enough cord to reach them. Locate the nearest rest room and exit in case of fire or other emergency. Ask your host for a pitcher of cold water and a glass.

You should have prepared shorter and lighter remarks if you are speaking after a meal when your audience will tend to be logy and even sleepy. Now it is time to prepare your body by eating lightly but sufficiently. Protein such as peanut butter, tofu, eggs, cheese, fish, poultry, or meat will give your body the most long-term energy. Avoid candy, sweet or heavy sauces and desserts that do just the opposite. An hour or two before and during a meal, if one is served, do not drink coffee, tea, soft drinks or alcoholic beverages, but do drink plenty of water and have a full glass handy. The other beverages will dry up your throat and hinder your ability to be clear and articulate.

Remove any coins or keys from your pockets before you speak so you are not tempted to jingle or play with them. Likewise, unless you are using them for emphasis, avoid having a pen or pencil nearby lest you tap and distract the audience. If there is no speaker's stand, have a table close on which to put your speech so that you can slide each page to one side unobtrusively.

Although you should have sent the host your current biographical sketch, bring along another in the likelihood t he or she has neglected to take it to the event and was planning to "wing it." In either case, by making sure the introductory remarks say just what you want said to this particular audience, you start off on the proper note.

After you are introduced, take as much time as you need to arrange yourself and your speech comfortably at the podium. Smile in a friendly way and look around slowly at the audience. It may seem like an interminable time before all those faces come into focus, but it will most likely be only a scant second or two. Be confident you are in charge and they have nowhere to go.

If there is a visible clock in the room, use it as your timepiece. If none is available, ask your host or a friend in the audience to give you a hand signal to apprise you when ten and then five minutes or so are left. Do not remove your watch or phone and lay it ostentatiously on the podium. That is a signal to the audience you are overly organized and unprepared for anything that will cause you to stray from your text.

If a few in the audience appear bored or distracted, do not waste your time trying to win them over by looking at them particularly or gesturing in their direction. Assume their disaffection has nothing to do with you or your remarks and is caused by a seemingly urgent text message or an argument with their boss, partner or spouse — in other words, nothing you can control. Concentrate your attention on the rest of those friendly and attentive faces.

Never, never exhibit your nervousness by starting your speech with a tap, tap on the microphone asking, *Is this on? Can you all hear me?* Such a gesture immediately brands you as a disorganized amateur who should have taken care of this beforehand and may not be taken seriously. As we have noted earlier, you should have tested the microphone beforehand to make sure it is working. If you are still uncertain, ask a friend or colleague to sit in the back of the room and signal you if the sound is too low or high pitched. Even the most state of the art equipment is known to wheeze and squeal at the least fortuitous times. If the microphone suddenly malfunctions, ask your host if it is easily replaceable. If it cannot be repaired easily and quickly, encourage people to move closer and speak loudly and clearly without it. The audience will empathize with the problem and appreciate your flexibility.

Speak without a mike only if it is not fixable or you are in a very small room. Speakers who eschew a working microphone by assuring an audience they do not need to be amplified can appear arrogant and risk annoying people who will be too polite to say they really are not able to hear.

Remember that a good sound system is not only sensitive, it can be dangerous. Never say anything within its range that may be confidential, even if you think you are whispering. And, as more than one public figure has found to his or her dismay, do not assume that when you think you have turned it off, it is actually off.

Do not drape yourself over the lectern

Stand tall, alert, natural and relaxed. Do not slump, move tentatively from one foot to the other, nor drape yourself over the lectern. Do balance yourself on both feet slightly apart and rest your hands on the podium, or one hand on the stand and the other in your pocket. As noted previously, before you get up to speak, remove all keys and coins you are likely to jiggle. Position your speech firmly in front of you.

Keep in mind you have just two minutes to capture the audience's attention before people are tempted to drift away. Your beginning remarks should be geared to this and so should your delivery. With sufficient preparation you will have memorized the first three or four sentences of your speech so you can concentrate on building that essential bridge to your listeners.

Your voice and facial expressions should convey a combination of warmth, friendliness and authority. Keep in mind you are an approachable, likeable human being with something important to say.

Vary the volume, letting your voice rise and fall in accordance with your message. If you shout nearly every word, your audience will not be able to tell what you believe is important; likewise, if you drone on and on in middle range, they will be bored. Whispers can be very effective in getting the audience to listen carefully lest they miss something important — but do not lower your voice more than once or twice or you lose the effect.

Avoid any nervous mannerisms that distract the audience from paying attention to your message. Do not take your eyeglasses off and put them on again incessantly. Using glasses as a pointer, for example, can be an effective gesture if not overused.

Do not concentrate on only a few of your listeners. Moving your head naturally from side to side, maintain eye contact with all of them. You can do this with ease only if you know your speech so well that you will not lose your place when you glance up.

If you do lose your place, relax and breathe deeply. Take all the time necessary to regroup. It may seem like an hour, but most likely it will be just a few seconds until you find where you left off. Do not worry about any negative reaction from the audience. They like you so well by now they will forgive-and may even think you planned- that pregnant pause. Avoid filling in your presentation with junk words such as *ah, er, y'know, right* or *okay*.

If your mind really does go blank and you lose your place or cannot remember what to say next, follow this advice:

> **Take a sip or two of water.** It has the salutary effect of lubricating your vocal cords and buying time until you can regain your momentum.

> **Keep talking even if you need to repeat what you just said.** The audience will think you are merely emphasizing an important point and never realize you have forgotten what comes next.

Keep moving. Step forward, backward, or to the side. One or two steps in any direction will get you going again. But, never turn your back to the audience.

Skip ahead to another part of your presentation that you do remember or can locate in your script. No one in the audience will notice except the few who may be taking meticulous notes. You should be sufficiently rehearsed and informed about your subject so you always have something to say. When you are off and running again, you can pick up the points you may have omitted.

Finally, no matter what has transpired, the time speeds on and you are near the end. Remember that second in difficulty to beginning the speech is finishing it well. If you have taken my advice so far, you have written a good, snappy, attention-getting conclusion.

Avoid the temptation to string it out by adding extemporaneous remarks because everything is going so well you have begun to enjoy the limelight. Say what you have decided to say, add a heartfelt *Thank you* and signify that you are ready for questions.

Savor the applause and attention. You deserve it.

Chapter 7: How to Answer Questions Without Catching Foot-In-Mouth Disease

Very few speeches are complete without a question and answer period. Consider it an integral part of your presentation — not an additional ordeal you are reluctant to undertake and hope to survive unscathed. If you handle the situation well, you should welcome the time as a further opportunity to get your message across, add ideas or information you were not able to include in your prepared remarks, help listeners clear up any uncertainties or ambiguities and enhance your reputation as a polished and accomplished speaker.

It helps if you are prepared when you are expected to be unprepared. As you write and rehearse your speech, analyze your audience. What do they probably know about the subject? What questions are they likely to ask? Jot down and memorize your answers and you will find at least some of these will be asked. This will help you to be somewhat rehearsed when you seem to be talking totally *ad lib*.

People ask questions for a variety of reasons: they were not listening carefully; they disagree with you and want an opportunity to express their own viewpoint; they are prone to pontificate no matter what the subject; or they sincerely want more information. Unless you know for certain that someone is eager to challenge you or is a proven windbag, assume that each individual has a genuine reason for asking the question and respond appropriately and politely.

Although the question and answer period should be somewhat informal, as the speaker, you are still in control. It should give you comfort to know you already have gained credibility by your prepared remarks and the audience is generally friendly and receptive.

When you finish speaking, the person who has introduced you should tell the audience you are open to questions but if she or he does not take the initiative, take it yourself: *We have a few minutes left. I will be glad to answer your questions.*

Start by setting a time limit for the entire question and answer period. It should be no longer than your speech itself and preferably shorter. Ask questioners to identify themselves; allow no one to ask a second question until everyone has had at least one turn (unless the second question is clearly a follow-up); and request questions, not statements. This is not the time for someone other than you to give a speech.

If you have sensed the subject is somewhat embarrassing or controversial, it may be prudent to ask for anonymous written questions. If so, allow about five minutes for people to write them down and have someone help you collect and sort them out. Move ahead as quickly as possible as people can be restless during this lag time and you lose momentum. Sort them according to general categories so that you can move the discussion along: *We seem to have three questions on the same subject. I'll answer them all this w*ay...

Your body language is an important non-verbal way of communicating that you are open and approachable. Avoid negative reactions to questions with which you may disagree such as frowning, shaking your head, or crossing your arms over your chest. If you have been speaking behind a podium, move somewhat closer to the audience if you can do that while staying within range of the microphone, or, even better, use a portable microphone.

Lean forward and make eye contact with each questioner, as evidence that you are listening intently.   .

As you listen, make a quick appraisal of the individual's agenda and/or feelings about the subject. You are more likely to be able to do this if you have taken time beforehand to know the audience. For example, a query, "*Who is going to pay for what you propose?*" is likely to require a different or nuanced answer if it is asked by someone you know is the president of the local bank than if it comes from the leader of an anti-tax citizens organization. Your facts should be the same, but possibly presented with different emphases.

If many people are raising their hands, ease the tension by recognizing

Do not fear a challenge from the floor

two or three you will call on in order. *Let's take Jane's question next and then the gentleman in the blue shirt.* Talk to the whole audience, avoiding one on one dialogue that excludes everyone else. If the questioner needs more information, offer to see him/her afterwards. *I'll be glad to talk to you more about this after the meeting. Please see me then.*

Make sure everyone hears and understands the question. Repeat and/or paraphrase. However, you take a risk if you check back after summarizing a particularly lengthy question (*Have I summed it up correctly?*) and the questioner answers *"No."* Better to assume you have heard it correctly and move on to your answer and then the next questioner.

Relate your answers to the experiences or concerns of this particular audience or to previous points you or others have raised. Remember that you do not have time, and most of the audience does not have interest, in an encyclopedic response. A polite *yes* or *no* may not only be the most appropriate answer, but may evoke laughter or defuse a tense situation.

If there appears to be some misunderstanding about what you said, restate a point you covered in your main speech. However, never infer that the questioner is stupid or inattentive by saying, *As I said before...* as if you mean, *You should have understood the first time, but I'll repeat it so you'll get it now...*

Do not fear a challenge from the floor. If you are correct, stand firm. *We will just have to agree to disagree on this matter.* If you are wrong, admit it and move on.

Never argue, lose your temper, nor insult the questioner lest he or she gains the natural sympathy of the audience that until now has been on your side. Use humor to deflect run-on or quarrelsome questioners. The audience will respond favorably to your smiling answer: *You certainly have an interesting point of view. You and I probably could discuss this for another six hours, but I suspect most of us would like to go home before then...*

If you really do not want to answer the question, take a cue from successful politicians. Answer the way you want to, not necessarily how the questioner may expect. Then, move quickly to recognize someone in another part of the room.

Do not be afraid to say *Sorry, I do not know the answer to this*. Ask the questioner to see you afterwards to obtain contact information. Follow up promptly. Answer critical questions politely and firmly: *There obviously are several sides to this issue.*

Avoid falling for "red herrings" or baited questions. Maintain your poise and if necessary, repeat the points you have stated previously or explain your position in greater detail.

Refer a question you cannot answer to someone you know in the audience only if you have obtained permission beforehand. *I see Gerry in the corner. I know she has the answer.* Never surprise someone by expecting him or her to bail you out of a tough situation or you will surely lose a friend or colleague.

If you have chosen to roam the room with a portable mic, never relinquish the microphone. Hold it firmly in front of the questioner so that you are always in control.

When the question period is over, do not trail off lamely with *Thank you; I see our time is up.* Instead, end on a high note by summarizing the main points you want to emphasize. *Before we leave, I hope you will remember these three points...one, two, and three. Thank you so much. It has been a pleasure to be with you today.*

That wasn't so bad, was it? You have shown once again that you are open and friendly and well versed in your subject. Having disposed of your text, you have taken advantage of another opportunity to show your skills and experience and at the least, gained some new friends and allies.

Chapter 8: Brief Remarks that Say Something

So far, we have covered the basics and beyond about how to give a polished oral presentation when you are the focus of attention, that is, the featured speaker.

However, as a manager, executive, key employee, program chairperson or other individual with responsibility, you most likely will be given the task sometime—at a meeting, conference, social or other event—either of introducing someone who has center stage, or of making a few remarks before the main program.

This second banana role, which should take no more than five minutes, can be important in its own way. By setting the stage for what is to come, you can perfect another set of skills that require a considerable art: to say just the right words shortly and succinctly. Make the most of each opportunity by preparing carefully.

For each situation, always introduce yourself if there is a chance at least some in the audience do not know who you are: *Good afternoon, everyone. For those of you who may not know me, I'm...* (Include your title, if you have one), *your host today...* Or, if everyone does know you: *Good afternoon. I appreciate the honor of representing us here today.*

The most common occasions for brief comments and advice about how to tailor them to your advantage are described below.

WELCOME. You have been designated as the representative of a group to extend greetings to the guest speaker. Keep your tone as warm and friendly as if you were welcoming the person in your own home. You are, indeed, the host.

Begin with words about the appropriateness or significance of the occasion: *It is our custom each spring to sponsor a lecture from a person who excels in her field. Anita Adams more than exemplifies the highest standards in...* Use the person's full name at the onset; you can be more informal in the rest of your remarks if the occasion warrants.

Next, add a personal and/or biographical remark that gives the speaker credibility with this audience. Choose your words carefully. Avoid a long, boring list starting with birth that continues with everything the individual has ever done. Instead, hit highlights: *It is fitting that she speaks to us today, as her achievements are many. Just a few of them are... Please join me in welcoming...* (Lead the applause and then step aside or sit down)

FAREWELL. You may be speaking for yourself or representing a group in saying goodbye to someone. If you or the individual are leaving willingly, the audience expects the occasion to be somewhat sad and nostalgic. If you or the individual are not leaving under the most amicable circumstances, the situation requires finesse and tact, with no mention of animosities which may have caused the parting. In either case, everyone understands you are carrying out a ritual that is difficult under the best circumstances.

Talk only of superficial pleasantries, and if it is appropriate, of tasks accomplished and deeds well done. Wish the individual well in his or her new undertaking, even if you are secretly delighted the person is leaving. If you are departing from the position or situation under somewhat clouded circumstances, be gracious and behave as we learned as children...as a "good loser."

AWARD PRESENTATION. An individual is being honored or rewarded. It is a happy occasion, and the audience is in a positive mood. In this case, fulsome praise and exaggeration are warranted, and even expected.

If you are giving the individual a scroll or a plaque, paraphrase its contents; do not bore the audience by reading and possibly stumbling over the text word for word. Say something about the history of the award and the criteria for winning. Add additional laudatory information about the honoree and his or her accomplishments.

If you think it is necessary to introduce the judges who made the decision, check beforehand to make sure they want to be introduced; some would rather be anonymous or, in some cases, the award criteria insist on anonymity. If you are presenting a gift, do not embarrass the honoree with a package that is difficult to open. Make sure it can be undone easily.

If the award has been mislaid or not yet arrived, be prepared with something to present – at the very least, a nicely printed piece of paper. Never have nothing.

Lead the hearty applause and stand aside for the honoree to say a few words.

ACCEPTANCE. In this instance, you are the recipient of an award or honor. Even if a well-meaning friend leaked the news to you beforehand, if you are supposed to be surprised, act surprised.

Unfortunately, the demeanors of many Academy Award winners are examples of what not to do. Resist the temptation to share the honor by thanking everyone you can think of who helped you get where you are today.   In all probability, the audience does not recognize their names and as importantly, does not care. Do thank groups in general—*my family, my staff,* and one or two very special people . . . *my third grade teacher, Miss Able, who taught me the value of persistence*, or *my mother/spouse/partner, who believed in me when others did not.*

If the award has a substantial monetary value, tell the audience what you are going to do with it: *This will enable me to continue my work with the underprivileged in our community. Thank you all very much.*

If you had official advance notice you were to be given the award, prepare and memorize brief remarks beforehand. Be gracious to any losers.

INTRODUCING THE MAIN EVENT. This is a situation where the purpose of your brief remarks is to promote the credibility of the speaker, not your own. Even so, this does not relieve you of the responsibility of being organized and interesting. If the speaker bombs, yours may be the only words the audience remembers.

Tailor your tone to the occasion. If the speaker is a well-known comedian expected to entertain the group, choose remarks that are somewhat light and frivolous (but no jokes, please). If he or she is talking about a serious topic such as the dangers of climate change, be equally as sober in your introduction.

Avoid the trite and unbelievable: *Our speaker needs no introduction.* If that is true, why are you here?

Give the speaker credibility for this occasion by doing your homework. Request a written biographical resume in advance and prepare your remarks by embellishing the hard facts with humanizing information.

Divide your remarks into the same three parts as you would any speech – introduction, body and conclusion. Begin by capturing the attention of the audience: *There is ample evidence that civilization as we know it is in real danger if we continue polluting the environment as we do today...*

In the body of your remarks, talk about why the speaker is the right person to make this address at this time. Focus on the person's accomplishments pertinent to this occasion, but do not recite a full biography. If relevant to demonstrating his appropriateness to address

this audience, you can also share elements of a personal connection: *Jack (or Mr. Jones if this is a more formal occasion) graduated from high school right here in town before going on to advance studies in environmental biology that have won many awards. And he says if it weren't for his freshman science teacher he wouldn't be where he is today.*

Do not damn the speaker with faint praise - *He is so well known; nothing more I can say will do him justice* - nor embarrass him with too much flattery that seems insincere.

Indicate any honors he has been given which establish his legitimacy on this occasion. He may have been an Eagle Scout when he was a teenager, but unless this increases his stature as an adult with this particular audience, leave that out. End with any pertinent human qualities, such as interesting hobbies or special activities.

Avoid personal references: *I remember when Jack was in town last and we had a fascinating discussion about this same subject. In fact, it is my opinion that...*This not only is of no interest to your audience but may get them wondering *Who does she think she is? We didn't come to hear what she thinks.*

Conclude with a simple but sincere statement: *We are honored to have such a nationally recognized expert in this field with us today.*

Compose your remarks and practice them, much as you would an entire speech if you were the headliner. If possible, use notes, not verbatim text you will be tempted to read.

Take care to pronounce the speaker's name correctly. If you have any doubt, check with the individual beforehand and write it out phonetically.

Lead the applause as the speaker rises; lead the applause when he or she finishes.

Decide beforehand whether you or the speaker will recognize audience questions, avoiding the awkward, *You first, no you first...*

As the question and answer period begins, detour an embarrassing silence by being prepared to ask the first question.

End on time with a pithy summary and a sincere thank you.

INTRODUCING A GROUP OF INDIVIDUALS AT THE HEAD OF THE ROOM. More gaffes probably are made in this type of oral communication than in any other. Is there a pecking order? Where should people sit? Which side of the table should be introduced first? How much should you say about each person? Organization and forethought will help you handle this situation with grace.

The following deals with the most common situations- either a formal banquet with one main speaker where you and special guests are seated at a head table; or a meeting or conference where you are behind a table with several speakers participating in a panel discussion. There is a third and growing trend in large meetings: to seat several speakers in comfortable chairs on a stage or platform.

In all these situations, you are responsible for introducing everyone and maintaining order in keeping with the occasion.

INTRODUCING THE HEAD TABLE BEFORE A MEAL. You are the convener of a group of eight, ten or more seated at the front of the room, with one main speaker.

First, it is important to arrange the seating. Facing the audience, place yourself immediately to the right and the speaker immediately to the left of the podium. Seated next to the speaker should be the most important person of the group...usually the president or chair, followed by other lesser sorts.   Any spouses/partners should be seated next to them, divided evenly on the right and left.

When most people have finished eating, or possibly during dessert, stand up, adjust the microphone and call the group to attention. You may have to resort to tapping a butter knife on a glass, but wait until most have settled down.

Introduce yourself: *Good afternoon/evening. I am (your name and possibly title if appropriate) and delighted to be your host for this special occasion. Before introducing our guest speaker, I want to tell you a little about the others seated at the head table.*

 A good rule to follow is from the outside in. Start at your far right and go down the line, saying a few appropriate words about each individual. Then, begin at your far left and do the same, leaving the speaker to the last.

Remember that nothing is more sacred to a person than his or her name. Be sure you pronounce each correctly. There are traps everywhere so check with each person, unless you know them very well. For example, does John Smyth pronounce his name as written, or *Smith*?

Ask each individual to remain seated as they are introduced, and the audience to hold their applause to the end. You may have to remind enthusiastic sorts of the latter more than once. Give each person, except perhaps the chair or president, equal billing, identifying title, rank or some personal but appropriate description. Save the speaker for the last, with a more detailed introduction.

Do not mix messages; be consistently formal or informal as the occasion requires.

Lead the applause for everyone before you come to the featured speaker. At that time, bite your tongue if you are tempted to say the trite, *Last but not least*. The last may or may not be the least. Avoid it. Follow the advice above for introducing a speaker; lead the applause once again and sit down.

Begin the applause once again when the speaker is finished but let him/her handle the question period, if there is one. Keep time and end on schedule.

TOASTING. There are many occasions — weddings, special anniversaries, birthdays, retirement parties — when laudatory remarks are in order. If you know in advance you will be called upon, prepare for it and follow the general formula in the section on introductions. As the occasion calls for wit and spontaneity, memorize what you want to say. This is one time in public speaking when hyperbole and exaggeration are acceptable and even appropriate.

Assuming there are other speakers or even if there are none, resist the temptation to run on interminably. Tailor your brief, memorable and meaningful remarks to the occasion.

If you are asked to give a toast at the last moment and are unprepared, a simple *Congratulations and best wishes, much success, etc.* is the safest and most appropriate response. The recipient and the audience will appreciate any brief, sincere comments you make.

ROASTING. Finally, this is an opportunity to have some fun. If you are the roastee, sit back and enjoy the silliness. If you are the roaster, keep your remarks succinct and in good taste. It is acceptable, and even expected, to be nostalgic and humorous: *We all know Hank as the upstanding citizen he is today but let me tell you a story about when we were both in the fourth grade...*

In summary, on those occasions when you are asked to make a brief presentation, have confidence you can rise to the occasion if you take each situation seriously. If you are told ahead of time, prepare and rehearse appropriately. If the situation is truly extemporaneous, you have enough experience to do a credible job. You may even find you enjoy this kind of speaking experience!

Chapter 9: Formulas for Impromptu Speaking

How often have we watched in awe as an individual gets up to speak after being asked unexpectedly to "say a few words" and then delivers an oration reminiscent of the Gettysburg Address?

Do you dread the possibility that you may be invited to make extemporaneous remarks at a business, social or other gathering? You can be successful if you heed the speech making skills you have learned in this book and the advice in this chapter.

At those times when the host or chair takes you aside just before the event, apologizing for the last minute request but nevertheless expecting you to agree to say a few words, do not demur modestly: *I really am not prepared. Perhaps you can ask someone else...*

Instead, nod and begin thinking about what you can add to the discussion that will be to your advantage. Take those few minutes to gather your thoughts, keeping in mind that although each of you is there for a purpose, you may not all agree on what that purpose is or what the results of the discussion may be.

When you are asked to speak, begin by complimenting the chair and the group: *Thank you for giving me this opportunity to say a few words. I know how important this is to all of us...* Follow this by referring to the remarks of some of the previous speakers. This shows you have been listening, not just waiting to express your own opinion. *As Jane just remarked...*

If the issue is somewhat contentious or controversial, take this opportunity to be the consensus-builder by summarizing what has been said and moving the discussion forward on your own terms. *It seems to me we have agreed so far on...Keeping this in mind, why don't we consider this course of action?* If you follow this format, and talk only about issues with which you are familiar, your brief remarks can positively advance your agenda and earn high marks from the audience.

Be calm on those few occasions when you truly are surprised to be called upon by the moderator: *I see Dana here and I know she* has *some ideas she would like to share...* The rest of the audience is probably relieved

Always be prepared to be "unprepared"

they have not been put on the spot when the chair points to you and are likely to be receptive to what you want to say. It will help if you have paid close attention to the conversation and possibly taken a few notes.

Do not decline to speak, apologize nor put down the chair by appearing modest. Avoid: *I never expected to be called on, but...*

Take your time. Move slowly to the front of the room or the podium, clear your throat, drink some water if it is available, and look around. Thank the chair for asking you all the while quickly assembling your random thoughts.

Begin with a compliment: *I appreciate being given this opportunity to say a few words because I know how important this subject is to all of us...In fact, this reminds me of the time when...*This is a good time to tell a story, preferably about yourself, that is apropos to the subject. If you are adept, quickly dredge up from your memory bank a similar situation or subject. Another technique is to refer to appropriate remarks of previous speakers. Finish by concluding with your own well-reasoned opinion. As before, talk only about those aspects of the subject with which you are familiar and look for the opportunity to bring about consensus or agreement on a matter important to you.

Avoid sarcasm and derogatory remarks, no matter how righteous you may feel.

In each of those situations that call for improvisation, keep to the subject and speak for no longer than five minutes. You will be surprised at how much you can say in a seemingly short length of time, and the audience will be impressed at how much you add to the quality of the discussion after appearing to be unprepared. If you ramble on and on they may become suspicious and wonder if you have a hidden agenda.

In summary, do not fear those rare occasions you are expected to make impromptu remarks. With careful attention, you will find they are yet another way of attesting to your credibility as a speaker.

Chapter 10: Principles of Effective Oral Presentations

This chapter is a summary of everything speakers need to be effective and successful.

A useful rule of thumb to remember is that the average attention span of an adult in an audience setting is 2/1/2 minutes, and in many cases less. That is equal to slightly more than the words on one double spaced typewritten page. Knowing this, it is important to keep the audience's attention by including discernable pauses and changes in tone and subject matter at appropriate intervals. Specific guidelines follow.

- ✓ **Before beginning to compose, ascertain the primary purpose of your presentation**: To inform? Convince? Entertain? Lead listeners to a conclusion? Anything else? Choose the context and content of your speech to meet that objective first, followed by others of lesser importance.

- ✓ **Tailor your remarks so they are likely to engage the attention of the majority of the audience** by being aware of at least these characteristics:

    - o Approximate number of people expected

    - o Average age

    - o Gender/ethnicity

    - o Occupations and interests

    - o Commonly held opinions or biases

- Known support of or opposition to issues you are covering.

✓ **Use words and phrases that will be easily understood** by this audience. Avoid jargon and esoteric or technical references.

✓ **Cover only three major ideas and help listeners keep track:** *My first point is...Second... In conclusion, etc.*

✓ **Do what comes naturally to you** – Stay away from jokes but do use humor or storytelling if and when it fits the subject and your personality.

✓ **Own your speech** - practice, practice, practice.

✓ **Prepare for the venue:** Ascertain beforehand the size of the room; whether the seating is open or assigned; auditorium or classroom style; table/chairs; microphone; other arrangements.

✓ **Control the territory**—come early to set up charts, electronic equipment and audiovisuals and make sure they work.

✓ **Be prepared when your mind goes blank**. Buy time by taking a sip of water, moving slightly, and/or repeating what you have just said: *I want to emphasize this point.*

✓ **Remember that people are persuaded by people, not by information.** If you are a credible carrier of information, your listeners will believe what you say.

✓ **Every speaker has butterflies**; those who are successful make sure they fly in the same direction.

Chapter 11: Fail Safe Checklist

After composing and rehearsing your speech to your satisfaction and before your presentation, test it by checking the following. Make adjustments as needed.

- ✓ **Does your overall tone and content assure the audience you are a credible conveyer of your message?**

- ✓ **Does your speech meet one or more of your specific objectives?**
  - ○ Provides useful information
  - ○ Elicits approval or support
  - ○ Helps promote understanding of a difficult or complex subject
  - ○ Deals with the subject with the appropriate tone
  - ○ Satisfies other important criteria

- ✓ **Does it meet the needs of the audience?**
  - ○ Avoids jargon and unfamiliar words and phrases
  - ○ Informs, persuades or entertains
  - ○ Keeps their attention and interest

- ✓ **Is your speech no longer than 20 to 30 minutes with:**
  - ○ Introduction that gets their attention
  - ○ Body with strong content that has no more than three main points
  - ○ Memorable conclusion

- ✓ **Have you rehearsed** until you are thoroughly familiar with the contents of your speech and are prepared when/if your mind goes blank momentarily?

✓ **Have you noted where to use gestures** and other means of non-verbal expression that are natural to you and will keep the attention of the audience?

✓ **Do your visual aids support your speech?** Do they neither overpower nor detract from your remarks?

✓ **Are your visual aids appropriate** for the knowledge level and interest of the audience -- and your skill in using them?

✓ **Is all your equipment in working order and do you or an assistant know how to operate it?** Do you have extra light bulbs and extension cords? Sufficient handouts, flip charts, pens, and other supplies?

✓ **Have you anticipated and rehearsed your answers** to typical or expected audience questions?

✓ **Have you checked the room beforehand** and will you come early enough to deal with any issues, such as:
  - Heating or air conditioner not working
  - Piped-in music (turn it off)
  - Electric outlets in inconvenient locations
  - Working light switch/dimmers
  - Seats arranged to your satisfaction
  - Podium or speakers stand where you want it
  - Microphone ready with correct volume and height
  - Drinking glass and pitcher with water
  - Contact information for building superintendent or maintenance person to help deal with any unanticipated crises

✓ About an hour before your speech, **will you have eaten lightly** and no caffeine or alcoholic beverages?

✓ Have you made **arrangements for close-in parking** so you do not have to spend valuable time driving around looking for a space?

✓ **Have you sent a biographical summary** or other material about yourself to the introducer ahead of time, and will you have another copy with you?

✓ **Do you have several copies of your speech** in case someone requests it?

✓ **Will you start and end on time?**

When you have answered a resounding YES to all the above, you are ready for a special experience.

GO FOR IT!

About the Author

For more than 40 years, Elaine Cogan has been the co-founder, with her husband, Arnold, of a national award-winning consulting firm in Portland Oregon. Elaine is a popular trainer and coach in successful communications techniques for business and professional people.

While engaged in her professional career, she was a host of a weekly radio program, columnist for the Oregon Journal and Oregonian newspapers and a political television commentator. As an ardent tea lover, she owned and managed a mail order tea company and has been celebrated at "one of the early founders of the modern tea revolution." Elaine has been honored as a Woman of Achievement by the League of Women Voters of Oregon; Woman of Influence by the Portland Business Journal; and a Woman of Vision by the Portland Daily Journal of Commerce.

In addition to the first edition of this book, she is the author of *Successful Public Meetings: a Practical Guide*; and *Now that You're on Board: How to Survive...and Thrive...as a Planning Commissioner.*

She was the first and only woman chair of the prestigious Portland Development Commission and also of the Board of Providence Medical Center in Portland.

Born in Brooklyn, New York, Elaine moved as a teenager with her family to Portland. She and her husband met when they were juniors in high school and married when they were juniors in college. They enjoy their three grown children, seven grandchildren and one great grandchild.